Hello, Family Members,

Learning to read is one of the most imp[ortant]
of early childhood. **Hello Reader!** boo[ks]
children become skilled readers who [...]
readers learn to read by remembering [frequently used words]
like "the," "is," and "and"; by using phonics skills to decode new
words; and by interpreting picture and text clues. These books
provide both the stories children enjoy and the structure they
need to read fluently and independently. Here are suggestions
for helping your child *before*, *during*, and *after* reading:

Before
- Look at the cover and pictures and have your child predict
  what the story is about.
- Read the story to your child.
- Encourage your child to chime in with familiar words
  and phrases.
- Echo read with your child by reading a line first and having
  your child read it after you do.

During
- Have your child think about a word he or she does not
  recognize right away. Provide hints such as "Let's see if we
  know the sounds" and "Have we read other words like this
  one?"
- Encourage your child to use phonics skills to sound out new
  words.
- Provide the word for your child when more assistance is
  needed so that he or she does not struggle and the experience
  of reading with you is a positive one.
- Encourage your child to have fun by reading with a lot of
  expression . . . like an actor!

After
- Have your child keep lists of interesting and favorite words.
- Encourage your child to read the books over and over again.
  Have him or her read to brothers, sisters, grandparents,
  and even teddy bears. Repeated readings develop confidence
  in young readers.
- Talk about the stories. Ask and answer questions. Share
  ideas about the funniest and most interesting characters and
  events in the stories.

I do hope that you and your child enjoy this book.

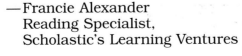

—Francie Alexander
Reading Specialist,
Scholastic's Learning Ventures

To my Rookie of the Year,
the fabulous Max Kraemer
— B.W.

For Matt and Alyse
— T.L.

Cover: Jed Jacobsohn/Allsport; Pages—4: Vincent LaForet/Allsport;
6: AP/Wide World Photos; 7: AP/Wide World Photos; 14: USC; 16: Duomo;
18: Otto Creule/Allsport; 22: Michael Zagaris/MLB Photos; 25: AP/Wide
World Photos; 29: Jed Jacobsohn/Allsport; 38-39: Brian Bahr/Allsport;
43: AP/Wide World Photos; 46: AP/Wide World Photos.

Text copyright © 1999 by Bruce Weber.
Illustrations copyright © 1999 by Thomas La Padula.
All rights reserved. Published by Scholastic Inc.
SCHOLASTIC, HELLO READER, CARTWHEEL BOOKS and associated
logos are trademarks and/or registered trademarks of Scholastic Inc.

Library of Congress Cataloging-in-Publication Data available.

ISBN: 0-439-09905-6

12 11 10 9 8 7 6 5 4 3 2   9/9 0/0 01 02 03 04

Printed in the U.S.A.   23
First printing, September 1999

Mark McGwire
THE HOME-RUN KING

by Bruce Weber
Illustrated by Thomas La Padula

Hello Reader! — Level 3

SCHOLASTIC INC. Cartwheel B·O·O·K·S ®
New York   Toronto   London   Auckland   Sydney
Mexico City   New Delhi   Hong Kong

I

Who Is Mark McGwire?

For one summer, he was the most famous man in America. He was more famous than the president. More famous than the most famous movie star. More famous than any other athlete.

It was the summer of 1998. That was Mark McGwire's summer of fame. Could he do it? Everyone wanted to know. Could Mark McGwire hit 62 home runs, the most in the history of baseball? Would he beat Babe Ruth's record? Would he beat Roger Maris's? The McGwire countdown was on every TV sports show. It was on every TV news show, too.

The record for home runs in one baseball season was, perhaps, the most famous in all of sports. In 1927, Babe Ruth hit 60 home runs for the Yankees. No one else even came close that year. Everybody talked about Babe Ruth.

Then, in 1961, Roger Maris hit 61 home runs for the Yankees. But by that time, the baseball season had gotten longer. Each team played eight more games. Roger Maris never got full credit for his record. So Roger and Babe shared the home run record.

As the 1998 season began, many baseball experts had one thought: Mark McGwire might be the man to beat both athletes.

Mark McGwire looks like he was built to break the home run record. He is 6 feet, 5 inches tall. He weighs 250 pounds. His muscles seem to have muscles. Fans call him Big Mac.

Big Mac is so strong, he scares some pitchers. What if he hits one back to the pitcher's mound? "The ball would probably go right through me," says one pitcher.

Mac doesn't see very well. When he isn't wearing his contact lenses, he wears very thick glasses. "Without glasses or contacts," says McGwire, "I can't see the top line on the eye chart!"

So who is this near-sighted, super-strong hitting machine?

Mark was born on October 1, 1963 in Pomona, California. He is the second of five McGwire sons. His brothers are Dan, Mike, Bob, and J.J. Mark's mom and dad had both played sports when they were young. His dad, John, was an excellent boxer. He later became a dentist. His mom, Ginger, starred on her college swimming team.

Dr. and Mrs. McGwire wanted their boys to try sports. And they did. In fact, Mark's older brother, Dan, became a great quarterback. He played for both the Seattle Seahawks and Miami Dolphins in the National Football League. Believe it or not, Dan is even bigger than Mark!

Mark played soccer before he ever tried baseball. Soccer was the number one sport in his neighborhood. He finally tried baseball when he was eight. Later, he played his first Little League game at the age of 10. In his first at-bat, he hit a home run. It was a sure sign of things to come.

But baseball wasn't the only sport Mark was good at. He may have been a better golfer than a baseball player. At Damien High School in LaVerne, California, he was also the starting center on the basketball team.

By his junior year, however, it was clear that his future was in baseball. He was an excellent pitcher. And he could hit like crazy. He always hit baseballs a long way. When he graduated from high school, he could have joined a professional baseball team. The Montreal Expos wanted him. But Mark and his family decided he should go to college first.

It was the right decision. In September, 1981, Mark went to the University of Southern California (USC) in Los Angeles.

When Mark got to USC, everyone thought he would become a great pitcher. But pitchers don't play in every game. They need to rest their arms between games. Mark's coaches wanted him in the lineup every day. So Mark became a full-time first baseman.

In his junior year of college, he hit 32 home runs. No one in USC's history had hit more than that in a *career*. Mark did that in just that one year! He certainly was ready for the pros.

But before he turned pro, Mark played for the 1984 U.S. Olympic Team. He got to play with lots of great players. They played practice games in big-league ballparks all over the country.

Mark was at the Olympic Stadium for the opening ceremonies of the 1984 Olympics.

At the Olympics, the United States team won all its games—except one! The Americans lost the gold medal game to Japan. It was an unhappy ending for McGwire.

After the Olympics, the Oakland Athletics—the A's—were waiting for him. They had picked him in the first round of the baseball draft. As a newcomer, a rookie, McGwire played in the minor leagues.

Mac played in Modesto, California.
He did very well. He was the California
League Rookie of the Year, 1985. It was a
wonderful way to start.

The star athlete moved quickly through the minor leagues. And, on August 20, 1986, he was sent to the majors. Only two years after his last college game, McGwire was in the big time in Oakland.

Mac's first full big-league season was 1987. He started slowly. But he really got going in Detroit in early May. He slammed five home runs in three games and it just got better.

When McGwire hit his 39th homer, he broke the all-time record for rookies. In fact, he set an all-time Oakland record with 49 homers. But he gave up his first chance for number 50.

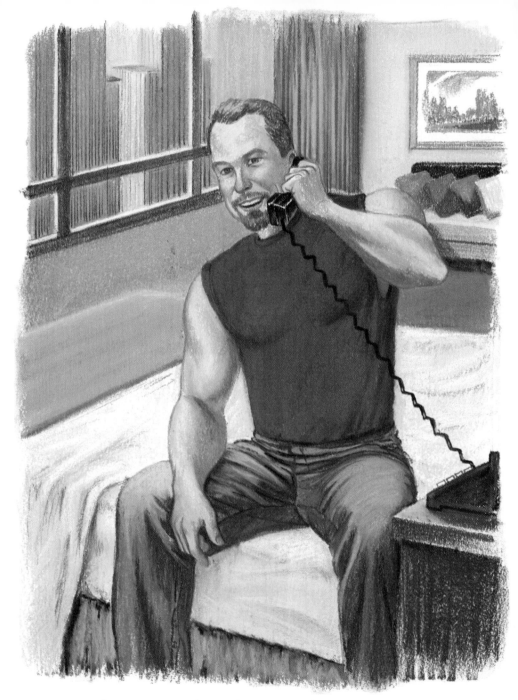

Mark was in the A's team hotel in Chicago.
In a few hours he would play against the
Chicago White Sox. But, he got a very special
phone call.

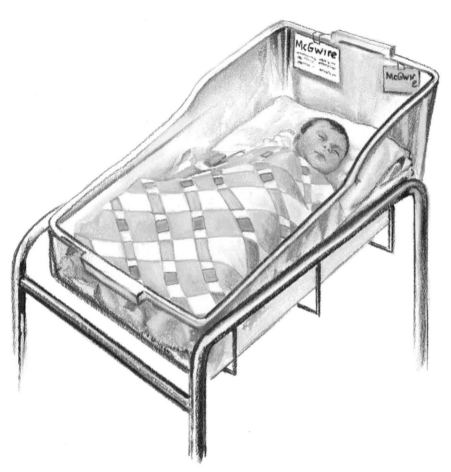

His wife, Kathy, was back home in Oakland, California. She was getting ready to have their baby. Mark left his team immediately. He flew to Oakland and rushed to the hospital. A few minutes later, he watched the birth of his son, Matthew. From that day, October 4, 1987, Matt became the most important person in his father's life.

"Hey, Matthew was my 50th home run," said Mark.

Two months later, McGwire was elected American League Rookie of the Year. He got every vote. It was a great way to end a great year.

Jose Canseco, Walt Weiss, and Mark McGwire were each once Rookie of the Year.

There were more highlights to come.
In 1988, Mac's Oakland A's made it to the
World Series. They lost. But Mac's home
run in Game 3 gave Oakland its only
winning game.

In 1989, the A's won the World Series.
They beat the San Francisco Giants in four
straight games. It was the most unusual
World Series ever.

The A's won the first two games at Oakland Coliseum. Then the Series moved to Candlestick Park 10 miles across San Francisco Bay for Game 3. A few minutes before the first pitch, the earth shook. Candlestick Park wobbled. An earthquake had rumbled through the Bay area.

Fires broke out in downtown San Francisco. Highways crumbled in Oakland. Part of the upper deck of the Bay Bridge fell onto the lower deck. Baseball fans and others watched on TV in horror. Suddenly baseball didn't mean very much. Game 3 was cancelled. Some officials asked that the entire Series be cancelled.

In the end, there was a 10-day break between Games 2 and 3. Then the 1989 World Series began again. Oakland won two more games—and the championship. It was a clean sweep.

The A's won the World Series again in 1990. Mark had 39 homers. But between 1991 and 1994, his game was hit and miss.

A bad heel injury wrecked his 1993 and '94 seasons. Again Mark bounced back. In 1995, he hit another 39 homers. No one in history ever had more homers in fewer tries!

In 1996, he did it again. He hit 52 home runs, an all-time Oakland record. The legend of Mark McGwire was born.

By 1997, the legend was on the move. The A's didn't have enough money to keep him. So in July of that year, they traded Mark to the St. Louis Cardinals. Mark was happy. He ended up with 58 homers for the season. Only Babe Ruth had ever had 50-plus homers in two straight seasons. Mark was now one of the all-time greats.

He signed a new contract with St. Louis. The Cards even promised Mark that his son Matt could fly on the team plane whenever he visited. Mark was really looking forward to 1998.

II

That Great Season!

Everyone in St. Louis was excited about the '98 season. At spring training, sports writers went to the Cardinals' manager, Tony LaRussa. "How many home runs can Mark McGwire hit?" they wanted to know.

"He could hit 40 or 50 or 60," said LaRussa. "Hey, if he gets lucky, he could hit 70!"

Nobody paid much attention to the manager. "70? That's ridiculous," most people said. But was it?

Big Mac didn't wait to start swinging.
In the first game against the Dodgers, he hit
a grand slam homer. The ball flew over the
left field wall, 364 feet away!

He blasted homers again in Game 2 and
Game 3 and Game 4. Only one other player
in baseball history had ever hit homers in
the first four games. That was Hall of Famer
Willie Mays, in 1971.

Then Mac went 10 days without a homer.
But when he broke out of his slump, he
broke out big time.

Mac's 10-year-old son Matt was visiting
from his home in California. That meant
Matt would be the Cardinals' bat boy. The
Cards were playing at home against a new
team, the Arizona Diamondbacks. In the
eighth inning, Matt's dad blasted his
longest homer of the year. It flew 462 feet
from home plate. It was McGwire's third
homer of the night and seventh of the year.
What a start!

McGwire kept right on going.

On the night of May 16, he came to bat against the Florida Marlins. McGwire smashed a fastball 545 feet from home plate.

It was the longest homer ever in Busch Memorial Stadium. It was the longest of the 1998 season. And it was the longest of Mark McGwire's career. "It was the best one I ever hit," he said after the game. "I don't think I can ever hit one any better."

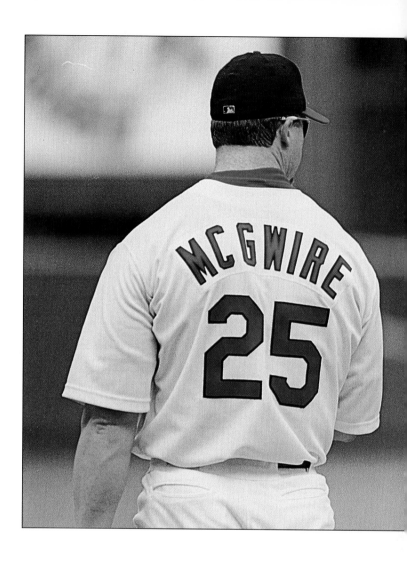

It was Mark's 16th homer of the season. And *then* he got hot! Before May ended, he had 27 home runs. In Chicago, however, another player was ready to give McGwire some competition. He was Chicago Cubs' Sammy Sosa.

By the end of July, Big Mac had 45

homers. Sammy Sosa was right behind
with 42. Mark and Sammy became the
talk of the country. Who would win the
race to get to 62 homers? Who would beat
Babe Ruth's and Roger Maris's record?
Excitement was growing about their race.
Baseball fever was catching everywhere.

Every game was sold out, long in advance. Fans started showing up hours before every game. Everyone wanted to see Mark McGwire hit a home run, even in batting practice. He rarely disappointed the fans. The seats in left field usually sold out first. That's where McGwire hit most of his home runs. All the fans wanted a chance to catch a McGwire home-run ball.

The left field seats at Busch Stadium were renamed Big Mac Land. It was the idea of McDonald's Restaurants. When Mac hit his first homer into Big Mac Land, McDonald's gave every fan a free Big Mac. That meant 47,549 free Big Macs. McGwire says he has never eaten one!

As September rolled around, the race continued. There weren't any questions. Either Mark or Sammy, probably both, would smash Ruth's and Maris's records. Which player would end up with more?

On September 5, in a home game, it was Mark who hit number 60 and tied Babe Ruth's record. "Babe Ruth! Babe Ruth!" Mark kept saying in the locker room. "I never dreamed I'd be in his company."

Two days later, Mark hit number 61—a 430-ft homer to left field. Mark caught Roger Maris and passed the Babe in the record book. When Mark arrived at the plate, his son Matt was there to greet him. Mark picked him up happily and held him high in the air.

Perhaps the happiest person in the stadium was Mark's father, John. The home run was a special birthday present for him. His son's 61st homer was hit on John's 61st birthday.

Now the whole country waited for the record-breaker—number 62. When would it come?

It didn't take long. Number 62 happened the very next night. It came in the fourth inning of a game against the Cubs.

The stadium went crazy. So did Mark. He was so excited that he forgot to touch first base. He had to go back and touch it. A few Cubs' players shook his hand as he moved around the bases.

When he got to the plate, the whole
Cardinal team was there to greet him.
He gave each one high fives and low fives.
He hugged everyone. He pranced around.
He jumped up and down. He screamed
and yelled. Fireworks cracked the
St. Louis air.

The game stopped for 11 minutes.
Mark hugged Matt. Mark hugged his
parents. Mark hugged Matt's mom.
He leaped into the stands to greet Roger
Maris's family. He even hugged Sammy
Sosa, who had trotted in from right field.
It was one of the most amazing moments
in the long history of baseball.

The season wasn't over, however. Sammy Sosa also topped Babe's and Maris's record. But McGwire finished the season as the all-time champ.

Amazingly, he finished with 70 home runs. The only person who had even thought about 70 was the Cardinals' manager, Tony LaRussa. And he wasn't really serious about it. Even Mac never gave it a thought. He had promised Matt he would try for 65. But 70? No way.

"I really can't believe I hit 70. Can anyone? It blows me away," said Big Mac.